Snips from Ei

MW01228337

Comprehensive Sexuality Education in the schools is pure propaganda for the Sexual Revolution. Protecting your child's innocence is your responsibility as a parent.

Dr. Jennifer Roback Morse – Ruth Institute

This book is a convenient tool to assist parents to benefit from the law of first mention—making sure your children hear things that matter from you first.

Dr. Andre Van Mol – Physician and speaker

A family-friendly tool parents can use to educate their children and help them navigate their way through a sexually saturated culture.

Dr. Michael L. Brown – Author and radio host

This book will help parents protect their young children from the lies that are ubiquitous in today's schools and found across all forms of media.

Dr. Michelle Cretella – Pediatrician and mother

The sexual revolution has led to childhood misinformation and root causes of depression, anxiety, self-doubt…the breakdown of the stable and loving family unit. This author reveals sound Judeo-Christian foundations about gender and sexuality.

David Pickup, LMFT – Reintegrative Therapist

This book is designed to help facilitate dialogue between parents and their children regarding human sexuality and relationships.

Susan Duffy – Co-Chair Protect Child Health Coalition

Too many classrooms are complicit in the rush to sexualize children from late elementary onward… That's why this book is so timely.

Linda Harvey – Mission America and radio host

Children are being bombarded with messages that are not age appropriate. Ellie's resources are backed by research and common sense.

Brenda Lebsack – Teacher and school board member

A book for kids and their parents that provides solid reasoning for waiting to engage in intimacy.

Caryl Ayala – Concerned Parents of Texas

A simple tool to show how sex fits into God's plan for our lives. Parents are directly responsible for sex education, and the parent determines when and where.

Jorge Tovar – Pastor and Church Outreach Coordinator

QUESTIONS FROM PARENTS

1. Is this a *birds-and-bees* book?

No, this is not a book about the physical act of "having sex."

2. What age child does this book address?

I can't say. That's the point. The parents are (or should be) the ones to intuit at what age their child needs or is ready for information relating to the whole subject of "sex." That's a good reason why the school should not be involved in early discussion of any aspect of human reproduction or "sex" in general.

3. Then what is the purpose of this book?

This book is a tool to help parents explain to their children in a simple way the place of "sex" in the context of God's plan for our lives.

4. But aren't children maturing physically younger these days?

Yes, children do seem to be maturing physically at earlier ages. Formerly puberty might begin at age 11 to 13 for girls but now may be as early as 9 or even 8. For boys, puberty formerly began at 12 to 14 but now often occurs at 9 to 12. But for many children, the older age is still common and completely normal.

Exposure to a sex-saturated culture is often confused with the issue of emotional maturity. But the question is not, "Are children nowadays exposed to more information about sex, as homogenized throughout our culture to stress sex appeal?" The real question is, "Are children maturing emotionally at younger ages these days?"

In my observance emotional maturity has not become more precocious. In fact, it may be the opposite. An over-emphasis on sexuality-as-central may be retarding the emotional development of children and young adults.

5. What should be the role of the school in discussing "sex"?

The school may introduce basic information about bodily changes to be expected at puberty, perhaps in late elementary years. Presenting this information in separate classes for boys and girls is wiser and much kinder to the children.

In middle school or later a biology class may cover basic human reproduction, *with limited graphics*, including information on the development of the baby in utero. Videos readily available show week-by-week development. This may impress students with the amazing sacred process of human growth in the womb, and the fact that "playing with sex" is not an option for children.

6. But what about informing children about the dangers of STI's (sexually transmitted infections)?

This would be included in science classes that deal with human reproduction, but the context should always be that sex within monogamous marriage is a very low risk factor for any STI.

An explanation of LGBTQ or any other aberrant sex behaviors is outside the purview of the public school and should not be included. No child should be forced to be informed about such. Any questions about this should be directed to the parents.

7. I don't want to talk about LGBTQ. My child is 7 and is asking where babies come from. What do I say?

For a four-year-old, the simplest explanation about "mommy and daddy loving each other and God put a baby to grow in mommy's tummy" may suffice.

For a seven-year-old, the simplest birds-and-bees explanation about a daddy part and a mommy part that together make a baby who is part of both of them may be all that is needed. Whether you need to include a basic explanation of how the daddy part joins the mommy part (with or without graphics) is a decision for each parent.

But keep it simple–don't overload your child.

For many children, the question may not arise or need to go beyond this for many years. The answer Corrie Ten Boom's father gave to her (see the back of this book) may be what is appropriate for your child.

So what's wrong with sex ed?
Don't we want kids to be protected from disease?

Did you know that –

– Comprehensive Sex Ed (called CSE) stimulates the early sexualization of children.

– CSE stresses your child's right to sexual enjoyment as soon as he or she "feels ready".

– CSE explains the "how" of LGBTQ sexual behaviors to young children, using graphic illustrations.

– CSE encourages a child to question his or her birth sex. This is called SOGI, for Sexual Orientation and Gender Identity.

Does this match your family values?

I hope this little book will help parents and children talk about their readiness–or their healthy reluctance– for public school sex education.

CSE lessons are now slipped into school subjects like math, art, reading, writing and history.

Is public school still the best option for your child?

RESOURCES

Check RESOURCES at the back of this book to see short descriptions and web addresses for articles and books cited on illustrated pages.

BUT I JUST WANNA BE A KID

A Conversation
Between Parents and Kids

Does Comprehensive Sex Ed
Match Your Family Values?

ELLIE KLIPP

Sex? when I'm ready?

Comprehensive Sex Education or CSE is telling boys and girls in public schools—even kids as young as third or fourth grade, "Sexual enjoyment is your right, when you feel ready."

Does this match your family values?

"The Legalized Sexualization of America's Young Children" – Marilyn Quigley

But I'm not ready. I'm just a kid.

A child 6 through 12 years old experiences a natural latency period when energies are directed to soaking up knowledge about everything from puppy dog tails and butterflies to multiplication tables.

"If you don't teach…" What is the latency period? – Leila Miller

I'm enjoying the innocence of childhood, a time to treasure and protect.

According to psychologists, a child who's exposed to sex information at the age of 4 or 5 may have delays in development.

From 6 through 12 years, a child exposed to sex education will frequently do less well in school, show a diminished development of compassion and conscience, and weaken the mental barriers controlling the instincts for modesty and restraint.

"A Psychoanalytic Look at Today's Sex Education" - M. Anchell
"NJ lawmakers, parents continue to fight…" – D. Matthau

If I have a question about sex, I'll ask my mom or dad.

Aren't parents the best judge of how much their child is ready to hear? Don't parents have the right to teach their *own* morals and values to their child?

Parents, do you know what's inside your child's books? Kids, what do you do if you hear something at school that is not what your parents taught you at home?

DeGroff, D. Between the Covers: What's Inside a Children's Book?

I don't need a boy- or girlfriend to know I'm an interesting and valuable person.

A University of Georgia study found that teens who did not date had better interpersonal skills, were less likely to be depressed, feel sad or hopeless, and were happier and more emotionally balanced than those who dated.

"Why Teens Should Wait to Date" – Isaac Khalil

I don't want to be in a class with both boys and girls talking about embarrassing stuff like puberty or what "having sex" means.

Did you know that Planned Parenthood is involved in writing most of the sex ed curriculums in the U.S.?

Is Planned Parenthood teaching your values?

"Planned Parenthood's Sexual Rights for Kids"– Child Protection
"Sexualizing Schoolchildren: Comprehensive Sex Ed" – Jeff Johnston
Brewer, Erin. *Transing Our Children*
Grossman, Dr. Miriam. *You're Teaching My Child What?*

At school, it's okay to teach basic biology and hygiene, but no "sex education" please.

Should schools push "consent" [grooming]
         or teach about conception [reproduction]?

King, Zach. *I Said NO! A kid-to-kid guide to keeping private parts private*
"The Clinical Steps To Grooming Kids…in Schools" - D. Housman
"Hi, my name's Olivia. Watch my story." - babyolivia.liveaction.org

I don't need to know about sex at my age. I'm way too young for romance or commitment.

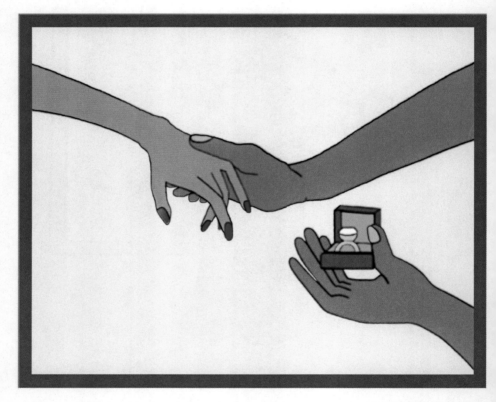

Young people who wait for romance are better able to finish their education. This leads to potential for better jobs and financial stability, which contributes to marriage stability.

"Why Teens Should Wait to Date" - Isaac Khalil
"But, Mom, we do love each other!" - Thomas Lickona

Commitment is a serious word. It means to promise, like forever!

The **ON** Dictionary

commitment - noun
1 a promise to remain true
2 a promise to be loyal
3 a promise to do something

Example: Marriage is a lifetime commitment.

Commitment requires the establishment of trust. That takes time. Making a commitment is a matter of honor.

"Six Reasons Why It's Still Smart to Wait Until Marriage" – Shelli Warren

Uh, would you want to spend your whole life with _____?

"Friendship Changes in the Teenage Years" – LIFE INSIGHT THERAPY

Dude, I'm still trying to make up my mind what flavor of ice cream I like best.

It's not just the flavor of ice cream that is a difficult decision for teens. A maturing brain and increased knowledge leads to new interests and shifting friendships.

"Understanding the Teen Brain" – University of Rochester Medical School

How could I possibly know what kind of person I like best? I'm just a kid.

I just wanna be a kid!

LET KIDS BE KIDS – "Introducing the Promise to America's Children"

I'll wait to have sex until I marry, like when I'm really old

like twenty or twenty-five or even older.

Studies show that couples who wait to have sex until marriage have happier and more stable marriages. In the teenage brain, the decision-making part is still developing.

"Benefits Of Waiting Until Marriage (& 3 Bad Reasons Not To)" – Catholic Match

God gave us boundaries for sex

'cuz sex by itself does not make you happy. Sex can make you ashamed, sad, and anxious if it isn't saved for that special person you will marry.

Studies show that early sexual activity undermines the emotional well-being of teenagers.

"Sexually Active Teenagers Are More Likely to Be Depressed and…" – Johnson et al

God wants us to be happy.

That's why it's God's plan to wait until marriage for sex.

"For I know the plans I have for you, declares the Lord, plans to prosper you and not to harm you, plans to give you a hope and a future." Jeremiah 29:11

"Let marriage be held in honor among all, and let the marriage bed be kept pure." Hebrews 13:4

Loving marriage builds decades of memories that trigger secret looks and smiles and jokes with your spouse, your best friend.

Sex is something wonderful for a man and woman to enjoy when married.

Having a lifelong partner means not only raising children and sharing the joys of life together, but also facing the trials and griefs of life together.

Maintaining a marriage is like a business commitment built on caring and respect.

God's recipe for a family starts with a mom and a dad. Then add a child or two or more.

Some children are added to the family by birth. Some children are added to the family by adoption.

Behold, children are a heritage from the Lord, the fruit of the womb is His reward... Psalm 127:3

"Top Ten Benefits Of Having Children" - Teresa McEntire

God made a family so a child is nurtured by the people who love him or her the very most.

Young children who grow with a secure and healthy attachment to their parents stand a better chance of developing happy and content relationships with others in their lives.

"Parent-Child Relationship—Why it's Important" - Blog on ParentingNI

Did you know that every baby is a "him" or "her" from the instant of conception?

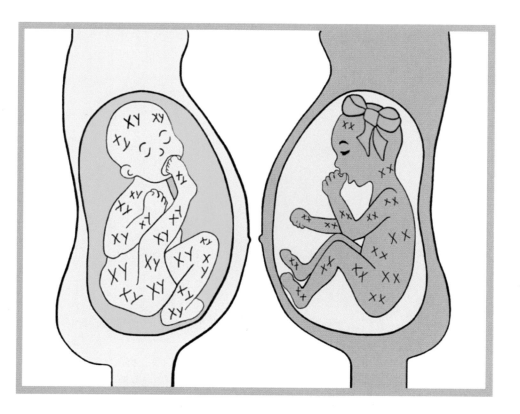

Each person in the world has 30 trillion cells, and each cell is coded XY (boy) or XX (girl).

"Conception: From Egg to Embryo Slideshow" -- WebMD

*Of course, this is a cartoon representation to make the point, not an actual depiction nor the correct position of a baby in the mother's womb.
** Each cell with a nucleus has a sex chromosome pair.

Some lucky babies have a Grandma and Grandpa, even two sets of grandparents.

Kids who spend a lot of time with grandma and grandpa tend to have fewer emotional and behavioral problems.

"Close Relationship with Grandparents Benefits Everyone" - Cleveland Clinic NEWSROOM

Other family members like aunts and uncles or cousins may impact a child's life.

There are benefits to having close family besides mother, father and children. But do all family members (and friends) model your values and behavior standards? Are there also risks?

"Benefits of being an aunt (or uncle)" -- Adera Robinson
Keffler, Maria. *Desist, Detrans, & Detox* (See pg 101 ff.)
King, Zach. *I Said NO! A kid-to-kid guide to keeping private parts private*
Shick, Denise. *What's Up with Cousin Stacy?*

But please don't keep talking about sex.

Despite our culture's obsession with sex, children and teens often appreciate being challenged to higher standards and healthier age-appropriate interests.

"10 Facts Every Parent Should know about Their Teen's Brain" - Nixon and Britt
Bevere, Lisa. *KISSED THE GIRLS AND MADE THEM CRY*
"Hobbies are Healthy" – Pam Meyers

I'm not ready.
I'm just a kid.

Loper, Tim and Ami. *THE MISSION: BOY TO MAN*
Young, Hal. *Raising Real Men: Surviving, Teaching and Appreciating Boys*

And I'm gonna go ride my bike!

Too Heavy for a Child to Carry

The Hiding Place is the story of Corrie Ten Boom, a young Christian girl in Holland whose father was a watchmaker.

During the Nazi invasion and occupation of Holland in World War II, Corrie and her family hid Jews in their home to save them from deportation to Germany and the death camps. Eventually the Ten Booms were caught. All but Corrie perished, but she survived the concentration camp horrors to bring a story of God's grace to the world.

Once a week her father, a master watchmaker, would travel by train about 18 miles from Haarlem to Amsterdam to pick up watch parts from suppliers there. Corrie loved to join her father on these trips.

The excerpt below is what Corrie wrote about one trip:

———————o———————

Often times I would use the trip home to bring up things that were troubling me, since anything I asked at home was promptly answered by the aunts.

Once, I must have been 10 or 11, I asked father about a poem we had read at school the winter before. One line had described "a young man whose face was not shadowed by sexsin."

I had been far too shy to ask the teacher what it meant, and mama had blushed scarlet when I consulted her. In those days just after the turn of the century sex was never discussed, even at home.

So the line had stuck in my head. "Sex," I was pretty sure, meant whether you were a boy or a girl, and "sin" made

Tante (Aunt) Jans very angry, but what the two together meant I could not imagine.

And so, seated next to Father in the train compartment, I suddenly asked, "Father, what is sexsin?"

He turned to look at me, as he always did when answering a question, but to my surprise he said nothing.

At last he stood up, lifted his traveling case from the rack over our heads, and set it on the floor.

"Will you carry it off the train, Corrie?" he said.

I stood up and tugged at it. It was crammed with the watches and spare parts he had purchased that morning.

"It's too heavy," I said.

"Yes," he said. "And it would be a pretty poor father who would ask his little daughter to carry such a load. It's the same way, Corrie, with knowledge. Some knowledge is too heavy for children. When you are older and stronger you can bear it. For now you must trust me to carry it for you."

And I was satisfied. More than satisfied, wonderfully at peace. There were answers to this and all my hard questions—for now I was content to leave them in my father's keeping.

THE HIDING PLACE, Corrie Ten Boom, with John and Elizabeth Sherrill. Fleming H. Revell Co. Old Tappan, New Jersey, c. 1971.

Some paragraphing changes added for readability.

Open-Ended Questions to Ask Your Kids
Maria Keffler - Advocates Protecting Children

Find out what's happening in your child's life by asking some open-ended (can't be answered with "Yes/No") questions.

Good rules of thumb for these discussions are to ask more questions than you make statements, and to listen more than you speak.

Another helpful trick is to ask questions about what your child's friends/peers are doing, rather than about what your child is doing.

Probing questions are less threatening when they're about others, and they also make a space for your child to "tattle" about something uncomfortable or scary that s/he may not have known how to bring up before.

1. What are your favorite songs? What do the lyrics say? Can we listen to one together? Are there songs your friends like that you don't? What don't you like?

2. What are you learning about relationships at school? What have you learned about families? What makes a family?

3. Do you ever see or hear about other kids using their phones in ways they shouldn't? What do you think are some of the benefits/drawbacks of having a smartphone?

4. Have you ever received an email or text that made you uncomfortable? What did you (or what would you) do about it?

5. Have you been told anything at school that seems to contradict what your parents have told you? How do you handle it when you get opposite information from two sources that you trust, like if two of your good friends told you things that didn't align with each other?

6. What do you think is a good age/circumstance to become sexually active? What are the benefits/drawbacks of becoming sexually active? What do you think we (your parents) think about sexual activity?

7. What do you think the main message of (book/videogame/movie) is? What is the worldview of the person who created it? How can you figure that out, just by paying attention to the dialogue and plot?

8. Is there anything going on that I can help you with? Is there anything that's scary or uncomfortable or confusing?

And no matter where the discussion goes, always end with, "I love you, and I'm always here for you."

Excerpt from Sex for Breakfast, Lunch & Dinner: A Day in the Life of a Kid in the U.S., Post by Maria Keffler on Advocates Protecting Children, 1-3-2022.

https://www.advocatesprotectingchildren.org/profile/e1914041-6973-418e-af16-d43934379d94/profile

Some paragraphing changes added

RESOURCES AND REFERENCES

ARTICLES

10 Facts Every Parent Should know about Their Teen's Brain – Robin Nixon and Robert Roy Britt. LIVE SCIENCE, March 31, 2016. Viewed 5-15-22.
A short analysis of the ways that a teenage brain is still physically developing and maturing during adolescence.
https://www.livescience.com/13850-10-facts-parent-teen-brain.html

A Psychoanalytic Look at Today's Sex Education - Dr. Melvin Anchell. American Life League's STOPP International. Viewed 1-16-22.
A doctor explains why sex ed classes in schools today from kindergarten through high school are so horrendously devastating, interfering with normal psychological development.
https://www.stopp.org/article.php?id=7206

Benefits in Delaying Sex Until Marriage – Bill Hendrick, Dec. 28, 2010. Posted on WebMD. Viewed 1-16-22.
More stable and happier marriages are among the perks, study finds.
https://www.webmd.com/sex-relationships/news/20101227/theres-benefits-in-delaying-sex-until-marriage

Benefits of being an aunt (or uncle) – Adera Robinson. Posted on SHARP Health News July 26, 2019. Viewed 1-16-22.
Aunts and uncles can provide a unique type of love and a positive role model.
https://www.sharp.com/health-news/the-benefits-of-being-an-aunt-or-uncle.cfm

Benefits Of Waiting Until Marriage (& 3 Bad Reasons Not To) – Posted on Catholic Match. Viewed 1-16-22.
The surprising finding of more compatibility if you wait.
https://plus.catholicmatch.com/articles/waiting-until-marriage

But, Mom, we do love each other! – Thomas Lickona. Posted on American College of Pediatricians website. Viewed 1-16-22.
How parents should talk about sex before marriage with their teenage children. Good things are worth waiting for.
https://acpeds.org/blog/but-mom-we-do-love-each-other

Close Relationship with Grandparents Benefits Everyone – Posted on Cleveland Clinic NEWSROOM, Sept. 5, 2019.
Research has shown that kids who get to spend a lot of time with grandma and grandpa tend to have fewer emotional and behavioral problems.
https://newsroom.clevelandclinic.org/2019/09/05/close-relationship-with-grandparents-benefits-everyone/

Conception: From Egg to Embryo Slideshow -- Reviewed by Brunilda Nazario, MD on November 15, 2021. Posted on *GROW* by *Web*MD. Slide 5. Viewed on 1-16-22.
At the moment of fertilization, the baby's genetic makeup is complete, including whether it's a boy or girl.
https://www.webmd.com/baby/ss/slideshow-conception

Friendship Changes in the Teenage Years – Posted on LIFE INSIGHT THERAPY COLLECTIVE, Sept. 16, 2021.
Changing friendships is a normal part of kids growing up, but here are some signs to watch for.
https://life-insight.com/friendship-changes-in-the-teenage-years

Hi, my name's Olivia. Watch my story. - The Baby Olivia project provides a medically accurate, animated glimpse of human life from the moment of fertilization.
https://babyolivia.liveaction.org/

Hobbies are Healthy – Pam Meyers. Posted on Child Development Institute, May 6, 2013. Viewed 8-3-22.
A short discussion of the benefits of hobbies. Hobbies stimulate learning new skills, like playing a musical instrument, woodworking, sewing, photography, stamp collecting, or participating in specialized clubs (chess, etc.)
https://childdevelopmentinfo.com/child-activities/hobbies-are-healthy/

How some schools hide sex curriculum from parents - Capital Resource Institute. Posted on Oregon Faith Report, Nov. 17, 2021. Viewed 1-16-22.
If a concerned parent asks to see the curriculum being used in his or her child's classroom, school personnel may show a large binder but what the parent never sees is the flashdrive available only to the teacher.
https://oregonfaithreport.com/2021/11/how-some-schools-hide-sex-curriculum-from-parents

How To Build Parent to Child Relationships – Posted on American College of Pediatricians website, MARCH 9, 2020. Viewed 1-16-22.
As a parent you have a responsibility to be the one who nurtures and protects your child.
https://acpeds.org/blog/how-to-build-parent-to-child-relationships

If you don't teach your child about sex… What is the latency period? – Leila Miller post, Catholic Answers Online, 8-3-2017. Viewed 8-8-22.
Parents should be aware of the latency period [psychology], often called the years of innocence. "From the age of about five until puberty, children should be left undisturbed by too much information about sex. But if the latency period is violated by receiving explicit sexual information too early, parents must begin to provide carefully limited sexual information, usually to correct immoral and erroneous information."
https://www.catholic.com/magazine/online-edition/if-you-dont-teach-your-kids-about-sex-guess-who-will

Lansing diocese adopts gender identity policy consistent with biological sex - Catholic News Agency, Jan. 15, 2021. Viewed 1-16-22.
The Catholic Church teaches that the human person is a body-soul union, and the body — created male or female — is an integral aspect of the human person. Each person should therefore, should acknowledge and accept his or her God-given biological sex.
https://www.catholicnewsagency.com/news/lansing-diocese-adopts-gender-identity-policy-consistent-with-biological-sex-

LET KIDS BE KIDS – **"Introducing the Promise to America's Children"** – Family Policy Alliance. Viewed 4-10-22.
https://familypolicyalliance.com/press-releases/introducing-the-promise-to-americas-children/

NJ lawmakers, parents continue to fight back against sex ed mandates - David Matthau, 8- 24-22. Posted on New Jersey 101.5. Viewed 8-24-22.
Pediatrician says introducing elementary school children to sexual concepts is confusing and psychologically damaging. Teaching children about sexuality, gender identity and sexual activity at an early age can traumatize them and pose a medical danger. Fourth and fifth graders don't have the ability to figure out sexuality. And

teaching eighth graders about LGBT sex is saying those are okay options, which is medically dangerous.
https://nj1015.com/nj-lawmakers-parents-continue-to-fight-back-against-sex-ed-mandates/

Parent-Child Relationship – Why it's Important – Blog posted on ParentingNI, Oct. 25, 2018. Viewed 1-16-22.
Young children who grow with a secure and healthy attachment to their parents stand a better chance of developing happy and content relationships with others in their life.
https://www.parentingni.org/blog/parent-child-relationship-why-its-important/

Planned Parenthood's Sexual Rights For Kids - Posted on Child Protection League website. Viewed 1-16-22.
International Planned Parenthood Federation (IPPF) has a published 40-page manifesto called, "EXCLAIM! Young People's Guide to Sexual Rights" distributed worldwide by the United Nations. It describes PP's sexual agenda in our schools.
https://cplaction.com/gender-identity/planned-parenthoods-sexual-rights-for-kids/

Sexualizing Schoolchildren: Comprehensive Sex Ed – Jeff Johnston. Posted on The Daily Citizen website, Apr. 22, 2022. Viewed 5-17-22.
This is the first in a series of articles about how children–from pre-kindergarten on up–are introduced to sexual topics in school classrooms, often with crude or graphic examples.
https://dailycitizen.focusonthefamily.com/sexualizing-schoolchildren-comprehensive-sex-ed/

Sexually Active Teenagers Are More Likely to Be Depressed and to Attempt Suicide – Johnson, K., Noyes, L., and Rector, R. Posted on The Heritage Foundation website, June 3, 2003. Viewed 1-16-22.
Teenage girls who are sexually active are three times more likely (and boys two times more likely) to be depressed than teens who are not sexually active.
https://www.heritage.org/education/report/sexually-active-teenagers-are-more-likely-be-depressed-and-attempt-suicide

Six Reasons Why It's Still Smart to Wait Until Marriage – Shelli Warren. Posted on BeliefNet. Viewed 1-16-22.
There is a lot to be said for maintaining old-fashion values about sex.
https://www.beliefnet.com/love-family/relationships/galleries/6-reasons-why-its-still-smart-to-wait-until-marriage.aspx

Talking to Educators About a Concern - Eric Buehrer. 1-31-18, on Gateways to Better Education article index. Viewed 1-17-22.
If you would like a teacher to change an assignment, consider this four-step approach to discuss the issue with the teacher.
https://gogateways.org/articles/2018/1/31/talking-to-educators-about-a-concern

Talking to Teenagers about Sex and Values - Posted on American College of Pediatricians webiste, Dec. 30, 2019. Viewed 1-16-22.
As society pushes more messages towards teens and children, it is even more important for parents to teach their children clear values and facts about how to manage their sexuality.
https://acpeds.org/blog/talking-to-teenagers-about-sex-and-values

TEN Facts Every Parent Should know about Their Teen's Brain – Robin Nixon and Robert Roy Britt. LIVE SCIENCE, March 31, 2016. Viewed 5-15-22.
A short analysis of the ways that a teenage brain is still physically developing and maturing during adolescence.
https://www.livescience.com/13850-10-facts-parent-teen-brain.html

The Clinical Steps To Grooming Kids Match Exactly How They're Being Taught in Schools – Dylan Housman. Posted on Daily Caller, 7-29-22. Viewed 8-9-22.
This author states, "The most common tactics groomers employ are…introducing sexualized topics or imagery to kids, isolating them from their parents, and encouraging them to keep secrets."
https://dailycaller.com/2022/07/29/grooming-schools-education-sexual-abuse-children-transgender-groomer-drag-queen-story-hour/

The Legalized Sexualization of America's Young Children - Marilyn Quigley. Posted on TOWNHALL, Jan 04, 2022. Viewed 1-16-22.
A shocking article about what is going on in classrooms across the country with sex ed.

https://townhall.com/columnists/marilynquigley/2022/01/04/the-legalized-sexualization-of-americas-young-children-

The Sordid History and Deadly Consequences of 'Sex Ed' at School - Alex Newman. Posted on The Reisman Institute website. April 6, 2020. Viewed 1-16-22.
https://www.thereismaninstitute.org/external-articles/2020/4/19/the-sordid-history-and-deadly-consequences-of-sex-ed-at-school

Top 10 Benefits Of Having Children – Teresa McEntire. Posted on families.com website. Viewed 1-16-22.
A lifelong investment in happiness.
https://www.families.com/top-10-benefits-of-having-children

Understanding the Teen Brain – Reviewed by Campellone, J. and Turley, R.K. Posted on University of Rochester Medical Center Health Encyclopedia, 2022. Viewed 1-16-22.
The rational part of a teen's brain isn't fully developed and won't be until age 25 or so.
https://www.urmc.rochester.edu/encyclopedia/content.aspx?ContentTypeID=1&ContentID=3051

What is the latency period? "If you don't teach your child about sex…"– Leila Miller post, Catholic Answers Online, 8-3-2017. Viewed 8-8-22.
Parents should be aware of the latency period [psychology], often called the years of innocence. "From the age of about five until puberty, children should be left undisturbed by too much information about sex. But if the latency period is violated by receiving explicit sexual information too early, parents must begin to provide carefully limited sexual information, usually to correct immoral and erroneous information."
https://www.catholic.com/magazine/online-edition/if-you-dont-teach-your-kids-about-sex-guess-who-will

Why Teens Should Wait to Date - Isaac Khalil. Posted Dec. 2, 2019 on Life Hope & Truth. Viewed 1-16-22.
A University of Georgia study found that teens who did not date had better interpersonal skills, were less likely to be depressed, sad or hopeless, and were happier and more emotionally balanced than those who dated.
https://lifehopeandtruth.com/life/blog/why-teens-should-wait-to-date/

BOOKS

Bevere, Lisa. *KISSED THE GIRLS AND MADE THEM CRY*. Nashville: Thomas Nelson, 2002.

Lisa has written gracefully and persuasively the intentions of God's heart for purity in female sexuality.

Brewer, Erin. *Always Erin*. 2021.

When Erin was a little girl, two men hurt her. She thought she got hurt because she was a girl and if she became a boy, she would never be hurt like that again. But she learned how to love herself again, to know that no matter what, she was always Erin.

Brewer, Erin. *Transing Our Children*. Chicago: Partners for Ethical Care, 2021.

Parents who hold biologically accurate views on sex and gender are called abusive and transphobic. Gender therapists and doctors lie to parents, saying puberty blockers do no harm.

DeGroff, Deborah. *BETWEEN THE COVERS, What's In Children's Books?* 2022.

An "explicit content" label on the cover warns that this book covers in detail the sexual and vulgar messages that trusting parents and grandparents do not suspect lie within the covers of innocent-looking children's books.

Grossman, Miriam. *You're Teaching My Child WHAT? A Physician Exposes the Lies of Sex Education and How They Harm Your Child*. Washington, DC: Regnery Publishing, 2009.

Dr. Grossman exposes why the dead discredited founder of "sexology" has more influence on sex education than today's eminent neurobiologists, and how "sex educators" ignore medical fact, teaching dangerous politicized propaganda.

Keffler, Maria. *DESIST, DETRANS, & DETOX, Getting Your Child Out of the Gender Cult*. Chicago: Partners for Ethical Care, 2021.

While gender identity politics paints the family as an oppressor, this book provides a roadmap to help families navigate the perils of transgender indoctrination and bring them back to reality and safety.

King, Zach and Kimberly. *I SAID NO! A kid-to-kid guide to keeping private parts private*. Weaverville, CA: Boulden Publishing, 2020.

    Helping kids set boundaries for their private parts. Written from a kid's point of view.

Loper, Tim and Ami. *THE MISSION: BOY TO MAN*. Maggie Valley, NC: Biblical Standards Publications, 2010.

    In addition to discussing the physical changes of puberty, this book prepares boys to face the new challenges of a maturing body and mind within a sacred context.

Shick, Denise. *What Up with Cousin Stacy?* Livings Stones Ministries, 2020.

    This book explores one family's response to the news of a loved one identifying as LGBT.

Werner, Audrey. *10 TIPS ON HOW NOT TO TALK TO YOUR KIDS ABOUT SEX*. McKinney, TX: RHEMA Publishing House, 2017.

    Who is behind modern sex education, and does Scripture have any wisdom about how to approach the subject with our children? What should we say, or not say, and when?

Young, Hal. *Raising Real Men: Surviving, Teaching and Appreciating Boys*. Great Waters Press, 2010.

Opt-Out Forms

For parents who hope to protect their children from inappropriate lessons in schools, Opt-Out forms are a possible option. An example can be downloaded from Concerned Parents of Texas.

Go to concernedparentsoftexas.com
Select ACT NOW
Scroll down and click on Opt-Out Form

Endorsements

Comprehensive Sexuality Education in the schools is pure propaganda for the Sexual Revolution. Protecting your child's innocence, and providing them with information that is appropriate for them is your responsibility as a parent. Ellie Klipp's *BUT I JUST WANNA BE A KID* provides parents with references and ideas for navigating this all-important front of the culture war.

Dr. Jennifer Roback Morse
Founder and President of the Ruth Institute
Author of 6 books, including *The Sexual State: How Elite Ideologies are Destroying Lives and How the Church was Right All Along*
ruthinstitute.org

Ellie Klipp's *BUT I JUST WANNA BE A KID* wisely reminds parents and guardians that comprehensive sex education is to be judged by its content rather than the catchy title. Ellie's book is aptly subtitled, "A Conversation Between Parents and Kids," something that must be ongoing in every home. This book provides a convenient tool to assist parents to benefit from the law of first mention - making sure your children hear things that matter from you first, so they can be skeptical of what they hear later that may contradict it. Otherwise, let not those who have Caesar raise their children be surprised that they grow to be Romans.

Andre Van Mol, MD
Board-certified family physician
Co-chair, Committee on Adolescent Sexuality, American College of Pediatricians
Co-chair, Sexual and Gender Identity Task Force, Christian Medical & Dental Assoc.

On a regular basis, concerned parents contact our ministry asking, "What can we do? Our children are getting bombarded by sexual images and sexual messages at younger and younger ages, including all kinds of LGBTQ+ indoctrination. The schools are bombarding them too!" Parents now have a family-friendly tool that they can use to educate their children and help them navigate their way through a sexually saturated culture.

Dr. Michael L. Brown
Host of the Line of Fire radio broadcast
Author of *Can You Be Gay and Christian?*

Ellie Klipp's *BUT I JUST WANNA BE A KID* is an excellent tool that will help parents protect their young children from the harmful lies of the sexual revolution, lies that are ubiquitous in today's schools and found across all forms of media.

Michelle Cretella, MD
Pediatrician and mother
Past Executive Director of the American College of Pediatricians

The sexual revolution over the past 60 years has led to childhood misinformation and root causes of depression, anxiety, self-doubt, low self-esteem, destruction of the body and mind via promiscuity, the breakdown of the stable and loving family unit and compensatory addictions that become attempts to deal with this darkness. Many of these children and adults are in my psychotherapy office for healing. Political and educational forces are indoctrinating children with destruction at early ages using a guise of compassion.

Ellie Klipp's new book, *BUT I JUST WANNA BE A KID* is full of truth and real compassion that will help lead parents and children back to love, safety, reason, accountability, emotional maturity, buoyant self-esteem, an ability to love others and self with wholeness, and a solid sense of right and wrong. Everything begins with the home and family, and Ellie Klipp cuts through the complicated darkness into simple light that will help parents and children get back to and stay on course. This author reveals sound Judeo-Christian foundations about gender and sexuality. The book is packed with what parents and kids can not only learn, but what to do as well. This is a must-read for all families of any age.

David Pickup, Licensed Marriage and Family Therapist
Houston, Texas

Ellie Kipp's book, *BUT I JUST WANNA BE A KID* is a delightful must read in an age where children are being bombarded with adult material. This book is designed to help facilitate dialogue between parents and their children regarding human sexuality and relationships. Everyone who believes in the importance of childhood innocence and safety ought to be able to use this book to help kids be just kids. Bravo Ellie!

Susan Duffy, Co-Chair – PCHC
Protect Child Health Coalition
President, The Pearson Foundation of Hawaii, Inc.
Hawaii Pearson Place Team website: https://hipp.team

Today's American child is bombarded with inappropriate sexual messages throughout the culture. One place where they should be able to escape is at school, but too many classrooms today are complicit in the rush to sexualize children from late elementary school onward, and comprehensive sexuality education is the culprit. This is why Ellie Klipp's book is so timely and necessary. Every parent needs to re-engage with the mind of a child and grasp the harmful impact that early explicit messages will have on emotional, social and spiritual development. Klipp dissects these reckless messages and presents parents with the tools to gently explore them with their children. I highly recommend this book for all parents!

Linda Harvey, President - Mission America
www.missionamerica.com
Radio host, WRFD www.thewordcolumbus.com
Author of *Maybe He's Not Gay*
https://www.missionamerica.com/article/maybe-hes-not-gay/

Finally---a book for kids and their parents that provides solid reasoning for waiting to engage in the most personally bonding experience--intimacy. A victory for families everywhere!

Caryl Ayala, Director - Concerned Parents of Texas
Former Public School Teacher (20 years)
concernedparentsoftexas.com/

BUT I JUST WANNA BE A KID is a great short read, a simple tool parents can use to approach their own kids—with graphics to show how sex fits into God's plan in our lives, or use as parents' own personal resource. Parents need to be informed about what society is pushing on our children now at a very early age. This book should inspire everyone to "let kids be kids."

Parents are directly responsible for sex education, and the parent determines when and where. Deuteronomy 11:18-22 gives parents the responsibility for teaching their children about godly values. Proverbs 22:6 says, "Direct your children onto the right path, and when they are older, they will not leave it." Parents need to rise and defend their own children, and people with decent family values need to rise and defend children in general.

Jorge Tovar, Sr. Pastor, Jordan River Valley Church, Laredo
Church Outreach Coordinator South Texas
Church Ambassador Network
facebook.com/texasvalues

Ellie Klipp provides excellent tools for parents to protect their kids' innocence and gives practical tools on navigating these challenging times, when children are being bombarded with messages that are not age appropriate and contrary to healthy relationships. Her resources are backed by research, common sense and experience.

Brenda Lebsack
Public school teacher since 1987
School board member from 2016-2020
Founder of the Interfaith Statewide Coalition
Writes for Brenda4Kids.com

Ellie Klipp's ***BUT I JUST WANNA BE A KID*** captivates the beauty of innocence naturally in the mind of a child. With a "retro" vibe, the childhood condition of sexual latency is well established, providing evidence based examples of why waiting to open the door to sexuality is best. She also delineates the proper roles for parents and teachers, describing the protections needed in the school system. This book is timely and potent for parents to get the conversation started. Ellie's assumption of marriage is quite refreshing in a day where it is often overlooked and poorly modeled. Parents are the gatekeepers for their children and this conversation starter should be a great tool to build the family.

Marsha Metzger
Director, Choose Now Inc.
choose-now.org

Dedicated in loving memory to
Sharon Armke
for her passionate concern for the children
and for her early and enthusiastic
support for this little book.

With special thanks to Janet Teal for her
feedback and encouragement, and to Caryl
Ayala for her support and suggestions. Also
additional appreciation to Ana Bernal and
Monica Cline for their input and support.

Ellie Klipp is a retired school teacher and a writer.

After receiving her B.A. from Biola, she did graduate work overseas and at UCLA, then taught elementary and middle school in three western states. In 2017 she earned an M.A. from MIUD (Masters International University of Divinity).

Ellie and her husband enjoy living near their grandkids in the southwest.

See more of Ellie's books at
ellieklipp.com.

Made in the USA
Columbia, SC
20 October 2022